Why, Bly?

by Dottie Raymer
illustrated by Kersti Frigell

Core Decodable 80

McGraw Hill Education

Bothell, WA • Chicago, IL • Columbus, OH • New York, NY

MHEonline.com

Send all inquiries to:
McGraw-Hill Education
8787 Orion Place
Columbus, OH 43240

ISBN: 978-0-02-143384-1
MHID: 0-02-143384-4

Printed in the United States of America.

10 11 12 13 KOD 24

Bly likes her head in dry sand.
Her pals don't understand why.

"Why not lie in the sun?" asks Snake.
"I get too hot in the sun," Bly replies.

"Why not hang in trees?" asks Chimp.
"I can't hang in trees," Bly replies.

"Why not fly in the sky?" asks Eagle.
"I can't fly. I am too big," replies Bly.

"Is Bly too shy?" asks a child.
"I am not too shy," Bly replies.

"My head feels better in sand," explains Bly.